THE WILD WOMEN OF STEAMPUNK

An Adult Coloring Book
for Fun, Fantasy & Stress Reduction

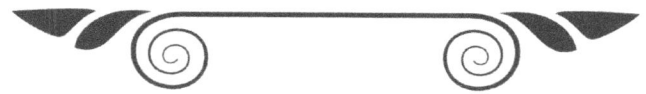

Curated By
STEPHEN WHITE

Foreword & Thrilling Commentary By
BYTUMENUS COLE

Copyright © 2015 Stephen White

Inner Hues - Volume 1

ISBN-10: 1517303397
ISBN-13: 978-1517303396

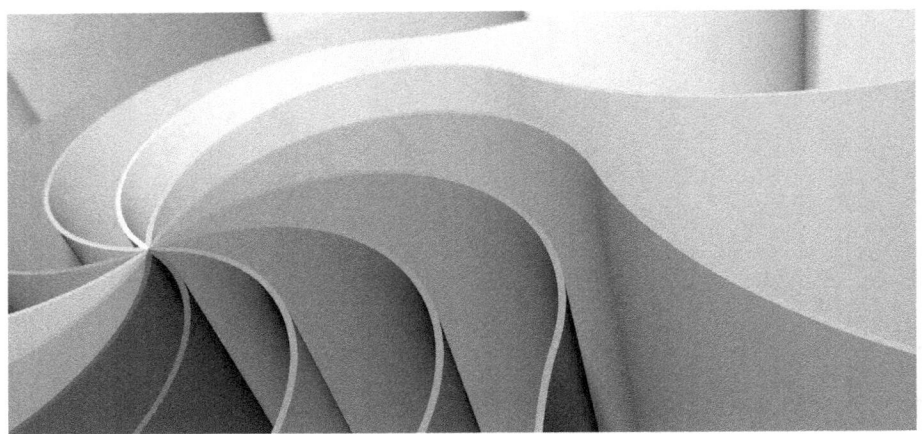

Soothing the "Inner You" with Inner Hues

Welcome to the *Wild Women of Steampunk* coloring book! We hope you'll have fun bringing these pictures to colorful life while imagining the thrilling adventures and derring-do of the lovely ladies assembled here.

We also hope and believe you'll enjoy the many stress-reducing benefits of coloring! The process is essentially a very simple and enjoyable form of meditation; a way to tune out the daily worries and distractions in your mind through the use of focused attention on an external task. Relaxation doesn't come from doing nothing. Rather, it comes from *actively engaging in an activity* which helps exclude internal and external stressors.

Choose the colors which please you - there are no wrong choices. Enjoy the feeling of accomplishment as you complete each portion of the picture. Let your mind wander as you explore this adventurous Steampunk world. We've given you some short story excerpts to get your mental gears turning but, just like the pictures, we've left plenty of blanks in these intrepid tales for *you* to fill in.

So clear the goggles and spyglasses from your desk, turn up your gas light, and put a disc of your favorite music on the gramophone (making sure to wind its mainspring first - you'll be here for quite awhile). It's time for you to begin your adventure in relaxation!

Free Bonus: *Steampunk Music!*

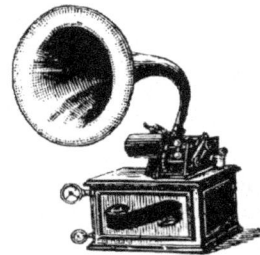

To enhance your coloring experience, we'd like you to enjoy a FREE mini-album of Steampunk music! Get your download now at **http://bit.ly/1SUPGCk**

FOREWORD BY
BYTUMENUS COLE

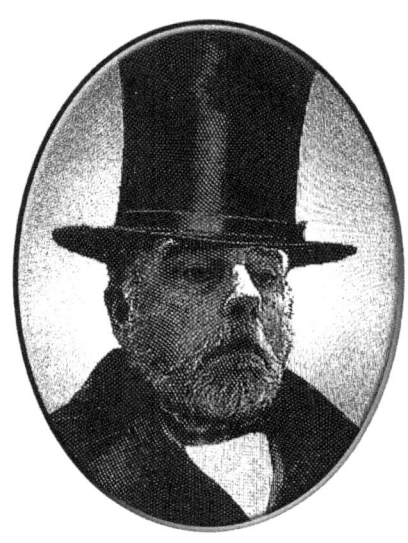

Those who are familiar with my recounting of remarkable true tales in popular literary journals (slanderously referred to as "penny dreadfuls") know that I have unparalleled experience in the observation and depiction of heroism, villainy, and the many remarkable changes wrought by our era's explosion of wondrous inventions and scientific advancements.

What has heretofore been unknown, however, is the extent to which the laughably-named "weaker sex" has entered the ranks of adventurers. These "wild women," if I may be so bold, are remarkably capable in every aspect: emotionally, intellectually, and physically.

They are also quite unconventional, not only in their choice of profession, but in their manner of personal presentation which can charitably be described as bold, but is more *frequently* characterized as immodest, risqué, brazen, and shameless.

While their choice of clothing is sometimes shocking to refined sensibilities and, indeed, common decency, those who remember the dread predations of the infamous Captain Nemo and his inventive ilk must applaud the intrepid courage of these distaff daredevils. To state matters bluntly, in times of peril a naughty lass is greatly preferable to a Nautilus.

Within these pages, I will introduce you to a full dozen fearless heroines and give excerpts from their breathtaking exploits. Do not doubt me when I state that, despite the perceived limitations of their gender, they are a match for any man. Those who were skeptical on this point have lived, and upon occasion *not* lived, to regret their incredulity.

-Bytumenus Cole

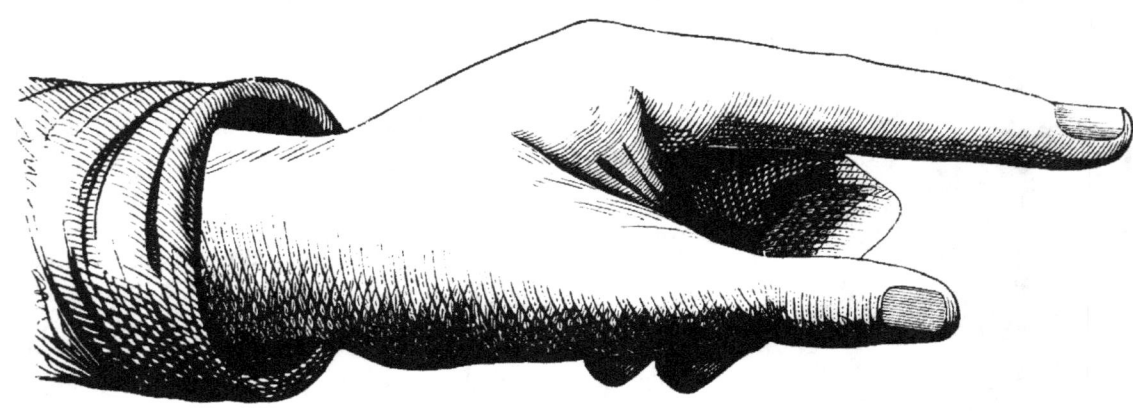

THE ADVENTURE BEGINS

ABIGALE

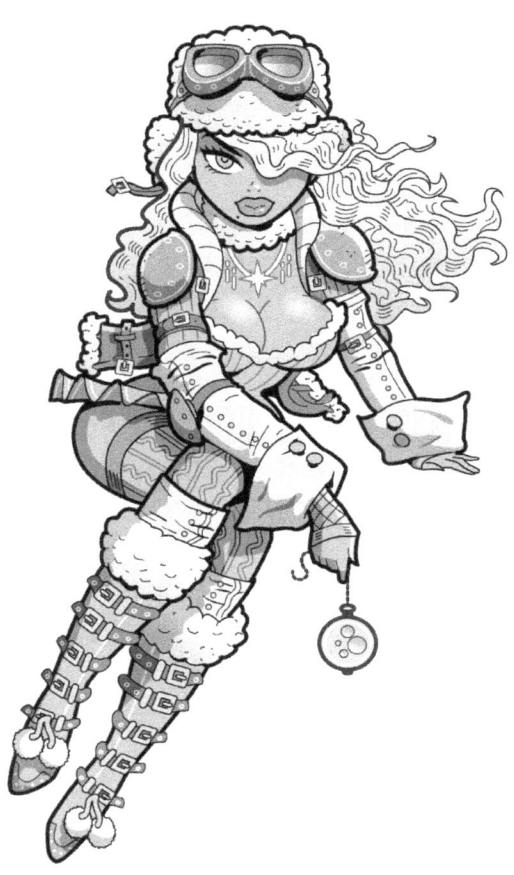

ABIGALE

"SORRY IF I TOOK YOUR SEAT," ABIGALE SMIRKED AS THE FURIOUS POTENTATE STRUGGLED FROM THE MARBLE FLOOR TO REGAIN HIS FOOTING. "IS THIS YOUR THRONE?"

"IT IS A THRONE WE MIGHT SHARE IF YOU ACCEPT MY PROPOSAL," THE POTENTATE ANSWERED. HIS GUARDS SLOWLY CONVERGED ON THE BRAZEN WOMAN, SCIMITARS IN HAND.

ABIGALE PULLED THE PIN FROM HER POCKETWATCH GRENADE. "ACTUALLY," SHE SAID, "I HAVE A COUNTERPROPOSAL."

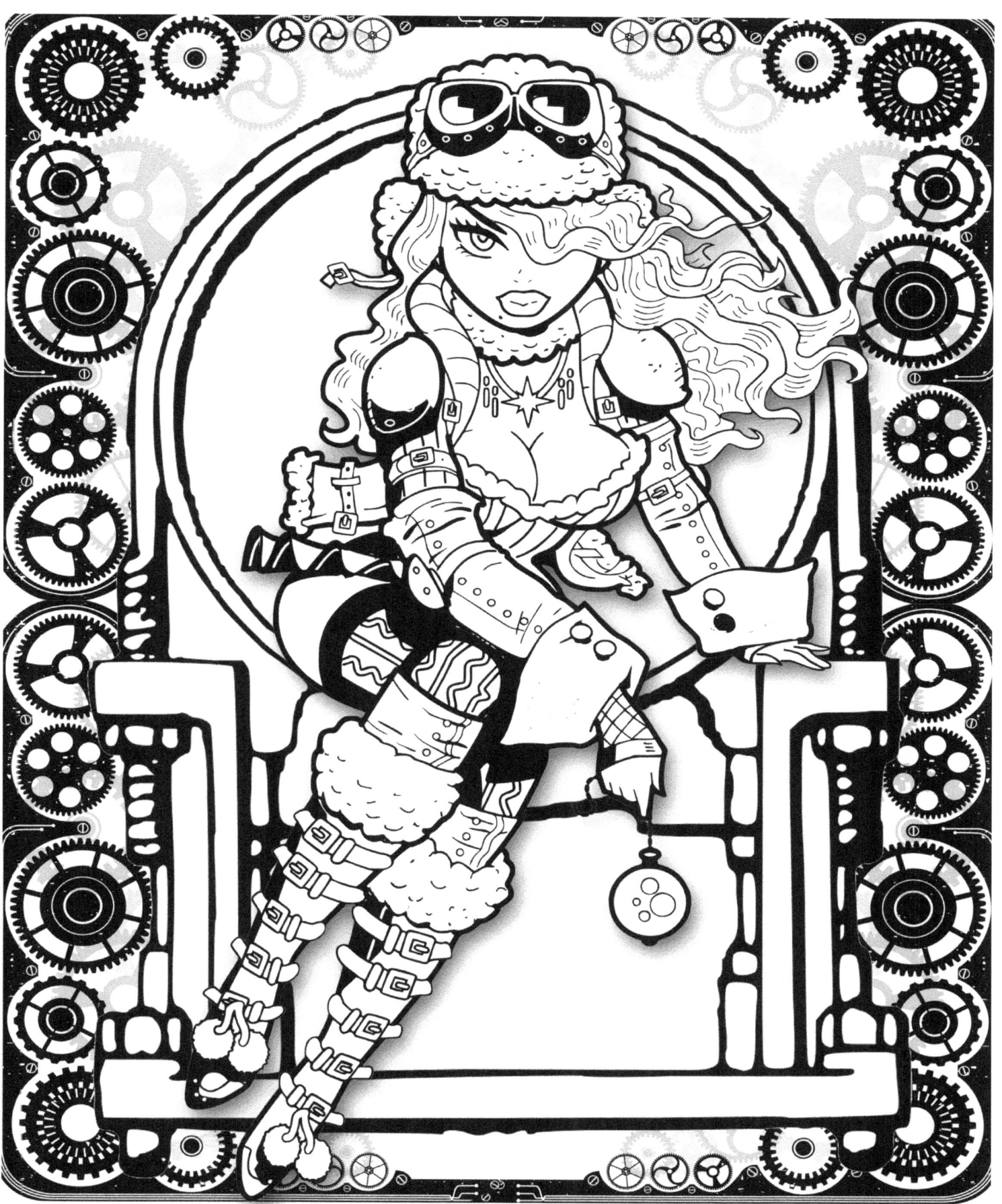

This page is intentionally left blank to prevent marker bleed through, and to let you remove your colored page on the reverse side for display

EDWINA

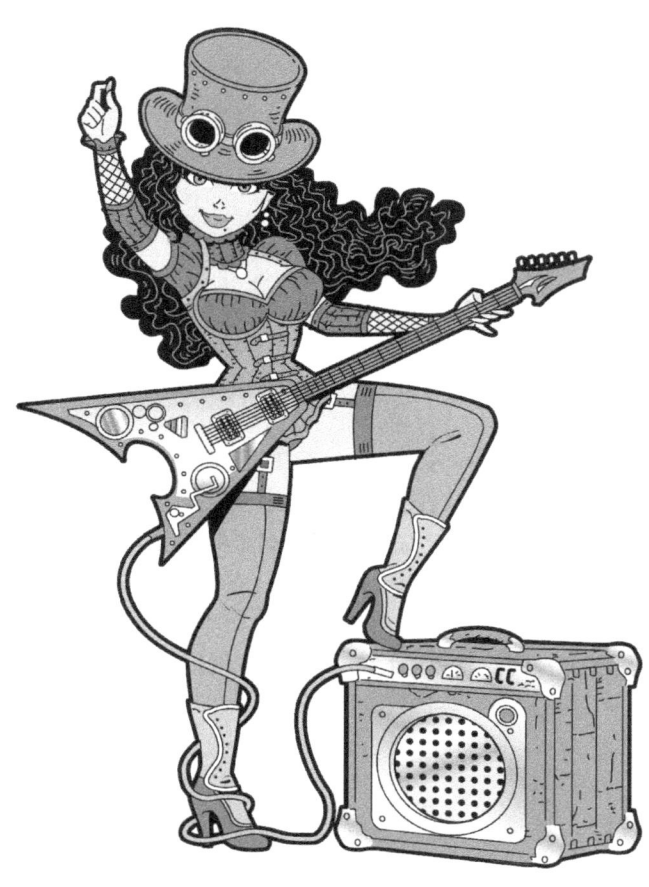

EDWINA

"THE SOUND, SO INTENSE AS TO SEEM A PHYSICAL FORCE, WAS UNLIKE ANY PREVIOUSLY HEARD IN NATURE; BY TURNS SOARING, RAGGED, BRUTAL, AND BEAUTIFUL.

SURROUNDED BY CLOUDS OF STEAM FROM THE SONIC MAXIMIZATION DEVICE, EDWINA ATTACKED THE STRINGS OF THE INSTRUMENT IN WHAT SEEMED LIKE A STATE OF FRENZIED ECSTASY. THE INVENTOR WAVED HIS ARMS, SHOUTING WARNINGS WHICH WERE LOST IN THE CACOPHONY.

"I WONDER," SHE THOUGHT, "WHAT MIGHT HAPPEN IF I TURN IT TO 11?"

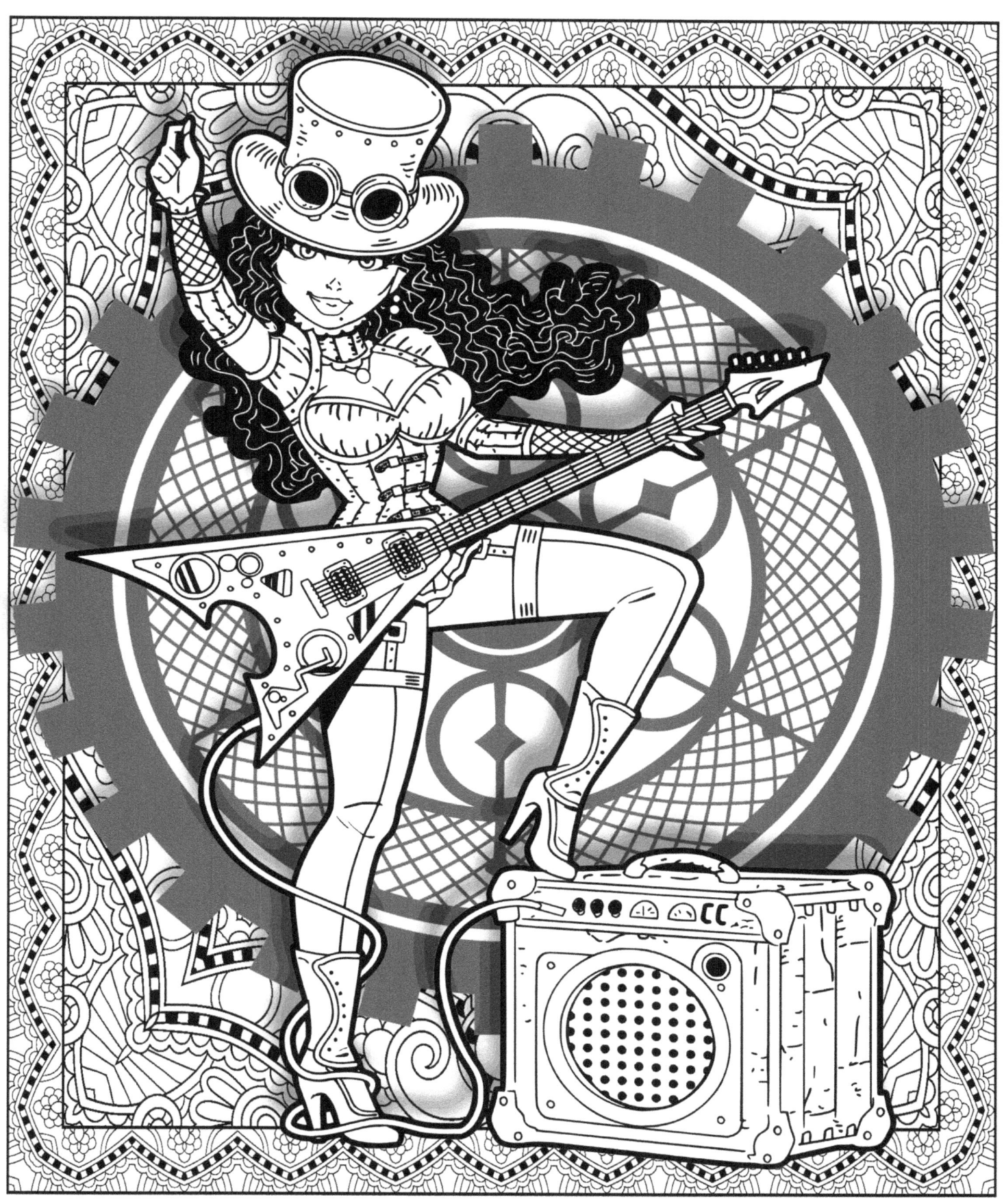

This page is intentionally left blank to prevent marker bleed through,
and to let you remove your colored page on the reverse side for display

MODESTY

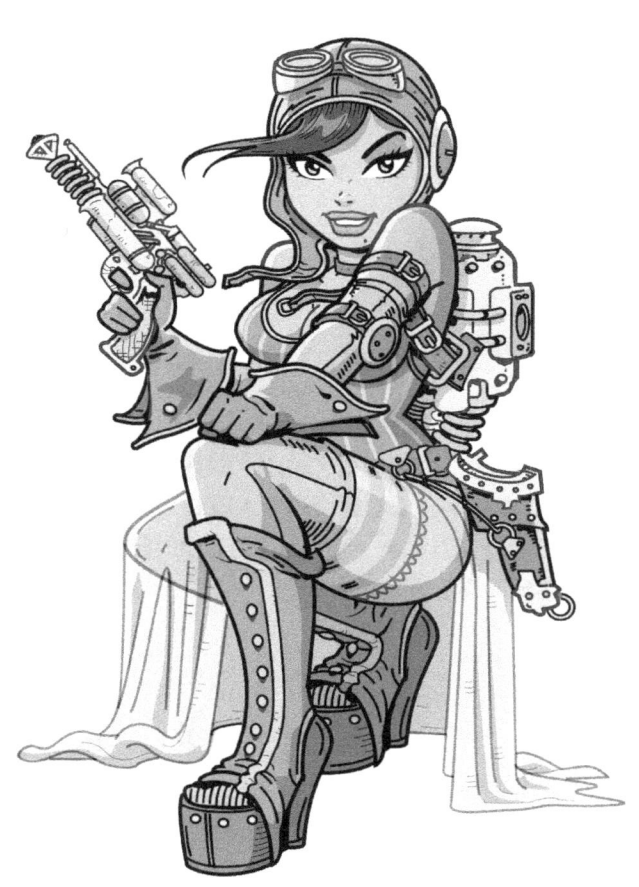

MODESTY

THE GROUND SHOOK WITH EVERY FOOTFALL OF THE METAL COLOSSUS, BUT MODESTY'S ATTENTION WAS FIXED ONLY ON THE PLASMA GUN IN HER HAND. THE ENERGY INDICATOR MADE CLEAR THAT SHE WOULD HAVE ONLY ONE SHOT.

"BUT THAT MAY BE ENOUGH TO TOPPLE THE GIANT," SHE SAID TO HERSELF AS SHE STOOD AND TOOK STEADY AIM AT THE MECHANISM'S ALREADY-DAMAGED KNEE JOINT. "AND FALLING INTO THOSE BLAST FURNACES SHOULD DO THE REST."

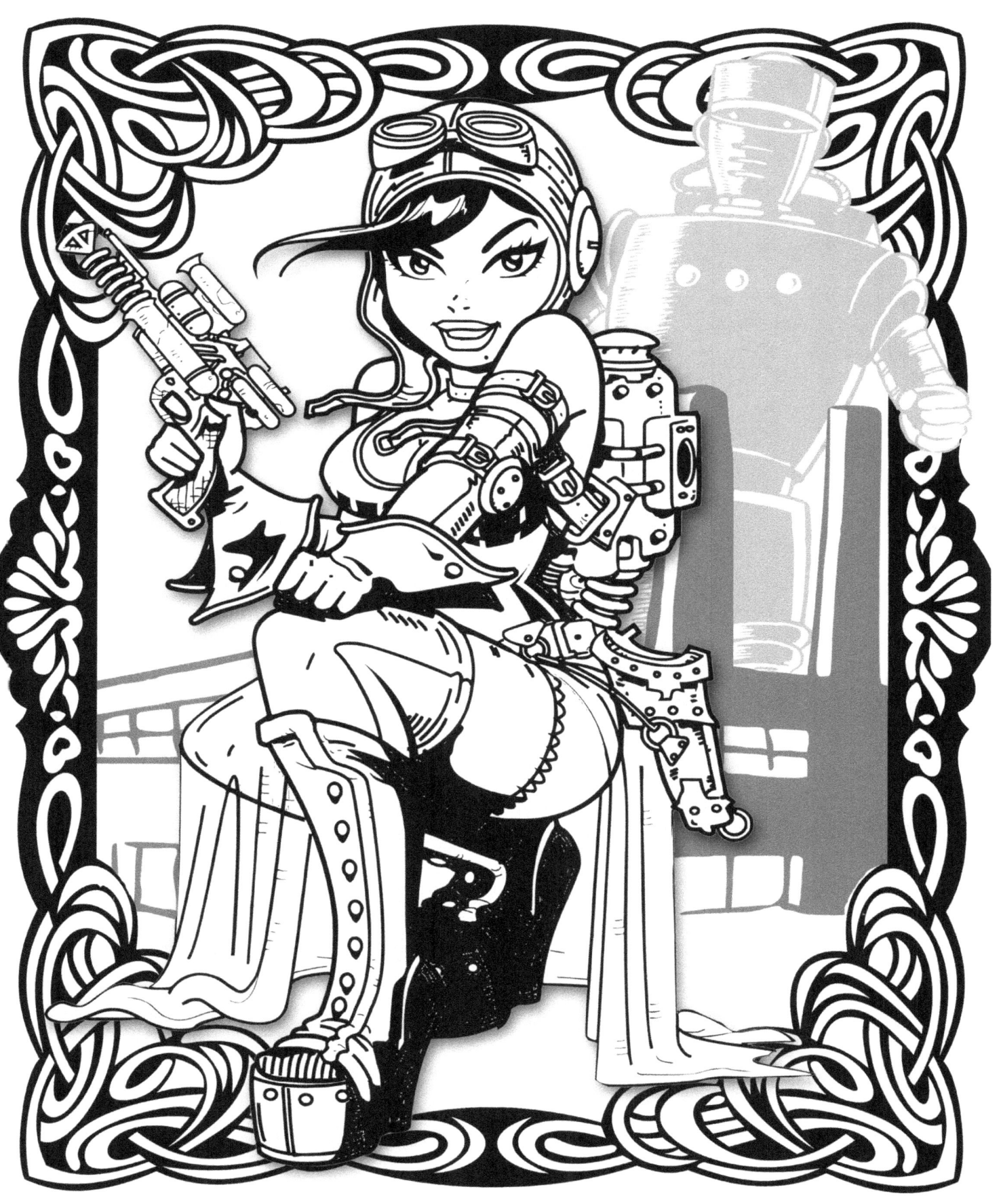

Maxine

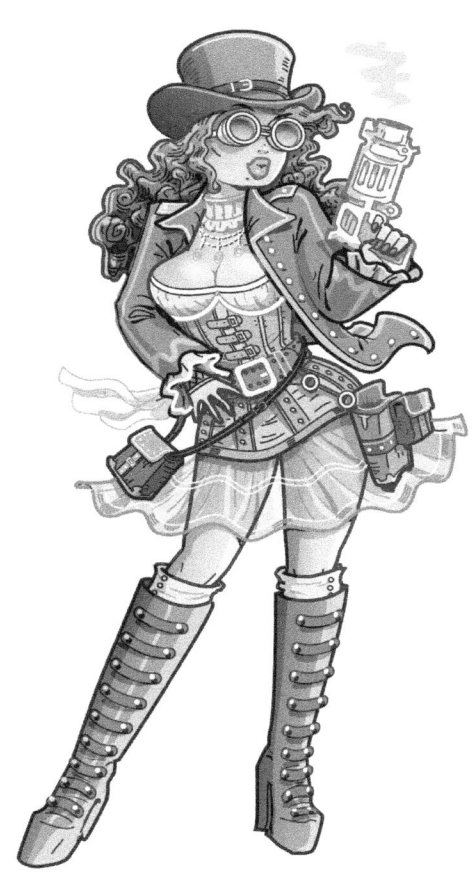

MAXINE

BEHIND MAXINE, THE NEEDLE ON THE HUGE COMPASS SPUN IN GREAT ARCS, STOPPING ONLY TO REVERSE COURSE AGAIN AND AGAIN.

"I NOW CONTROL EARTH'S MAGNETIC FIELD," SAID DUNORTH, "AND WITH IT, THE NAVIGATIONAL TOOLS WHICH ALL NATIONS RELY ON FOR COMMERCE AND MILITARY STRENGTH. MOREOVER, MY MASTERY OF MAGNETISM ASSURES THAT YOUR METAL BULLETS POSE NO THREAT TO MY PERSON."

"METAL BULLETS?" MAXINE LAUGHED AS SHE FIRED THE FLARE GUN.

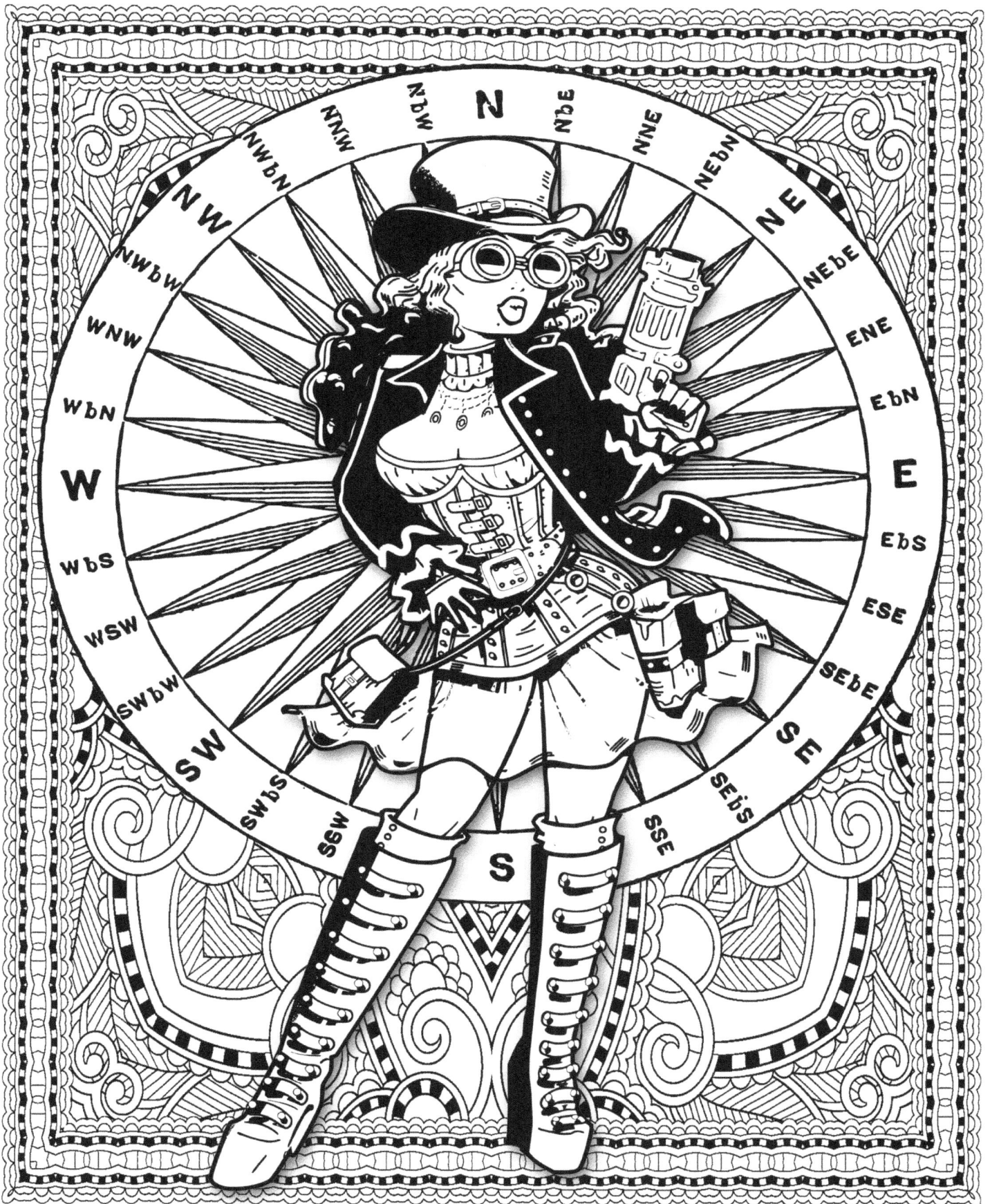

This page is intentionally left blank to prevent marker bleed through, and to let you remove your colored page on the reverse side for display

HORTENCE

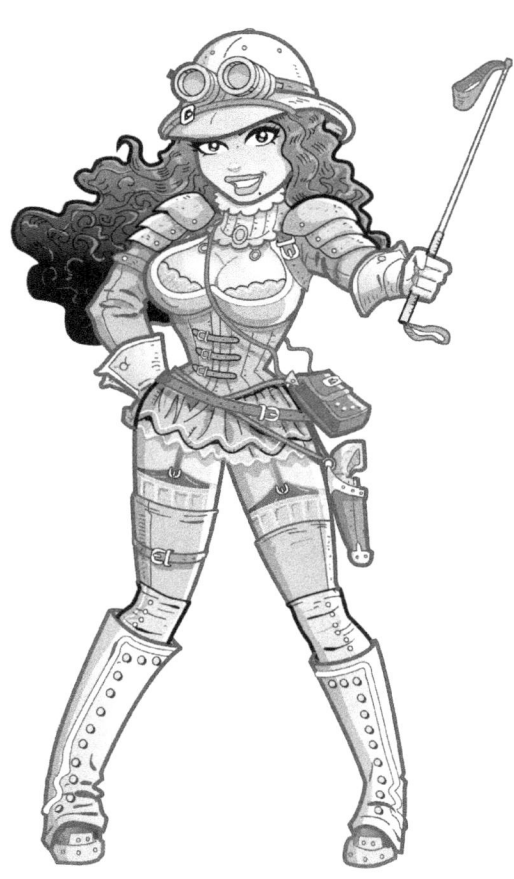

HORTENCE

The huge Bedouin tradesman was shocked when the beautiful woman impatiently jabbed her riding crop into his chest and addressed him in his native tongue.

"I need your fastest camel," Hortence said, "and I've no time for the pleasures of bargaining. I will pay twice what the beast is worth, assuming that you'll accept diamonds."

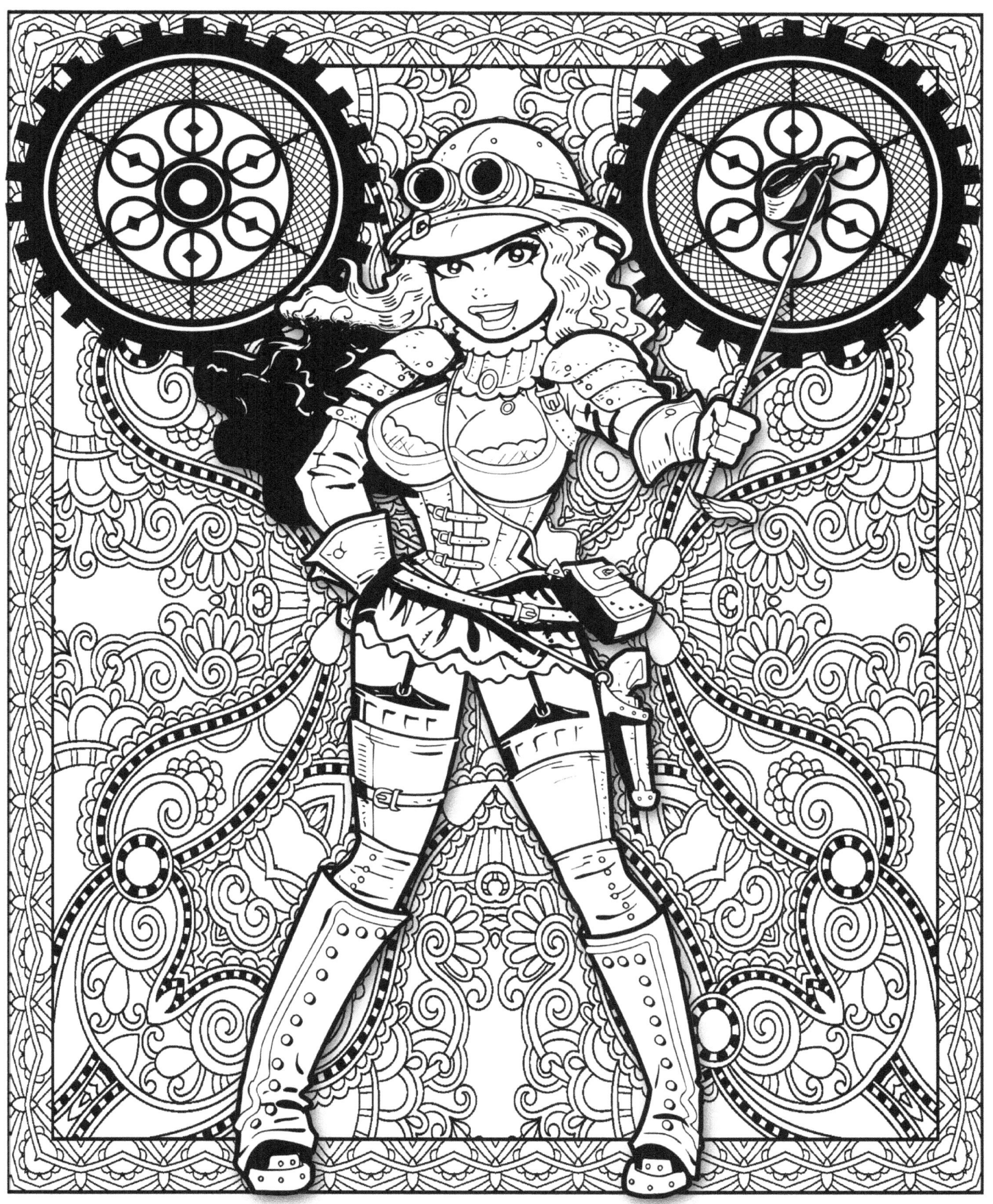

This page is intentionally left blank to prevent marker bleed through, and to let you remove your colored page on the reverse side for display

Sarah

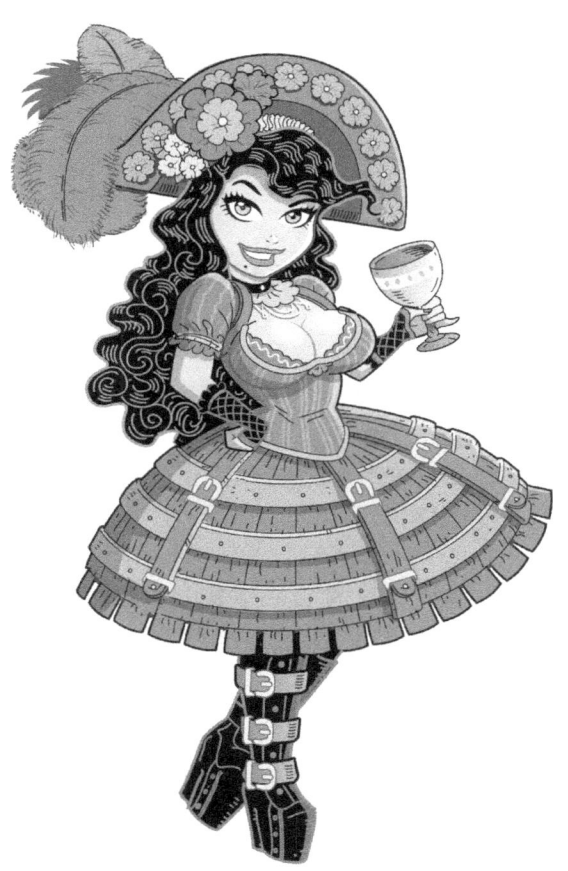

SARAH

"ARE YOU ENJOYING THE WINE?" ASKED THE BARON, A DISTINCT NOTE OF PUZZLEMENT IN HIS VOICE.

"QUITE," SARAH ANSWERED, DRAINING HER GLASS. "THE POISON WOULD PROBABLY BE UNDETECTABLE TO ANYONE LACKING MY EXPERTISE IN TOXINS AND QUITE FATAL TO ANYONE WHO HADN'T SPENT A LIFETIME CULTIVATING COMPLETE IMMUNITY."

"BUT ENOUGH ABOUT ME," SHE CONTINUED. "LET'S TALK ABOUT YOU. AND WHAT YOU MUST DO QUICKLY TO OBTAIN THE ANTIDOTE TO THE POISON WHICH I PUT IN *YOUR* GLASS."

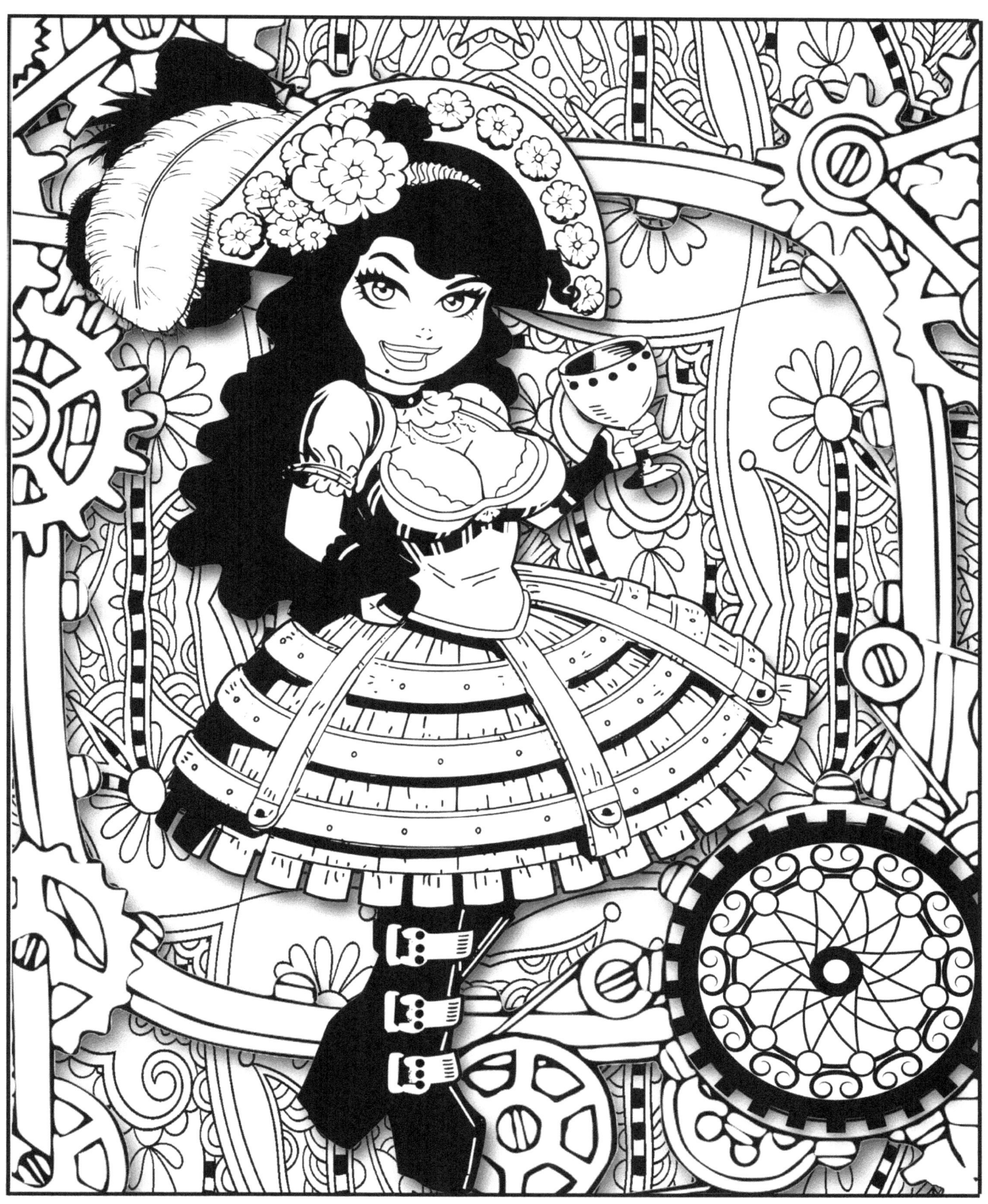

This page is intentionally left blank to prevent marker bleed through, and to let you remove your colored page on the reverse side for display

Theodosia

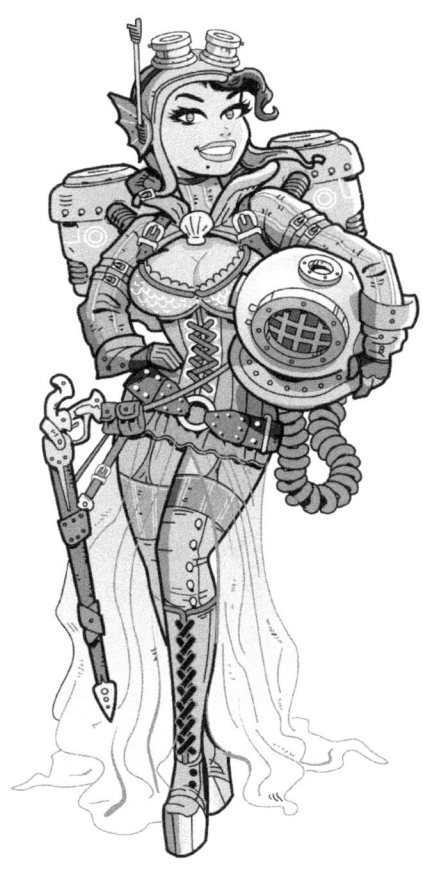

THEODOSIA

"ATLANTIS OWES YOU A GREAT DEBT," SAID THE HIGH PRIEST. "HOW CAN WE EVER REPAY YOU?"

THEODOSIA LIFTED HER ATMOSPHERIC HELMET AND ANSWERED WITHOUT HESITATION.

"LEND ME A FULL COMPLEMENT OF YOUR BRAVEST WHALERIDERS. IT IS TIME FOR US TO STRIKE DOWN OUR COMMON ENEMY."

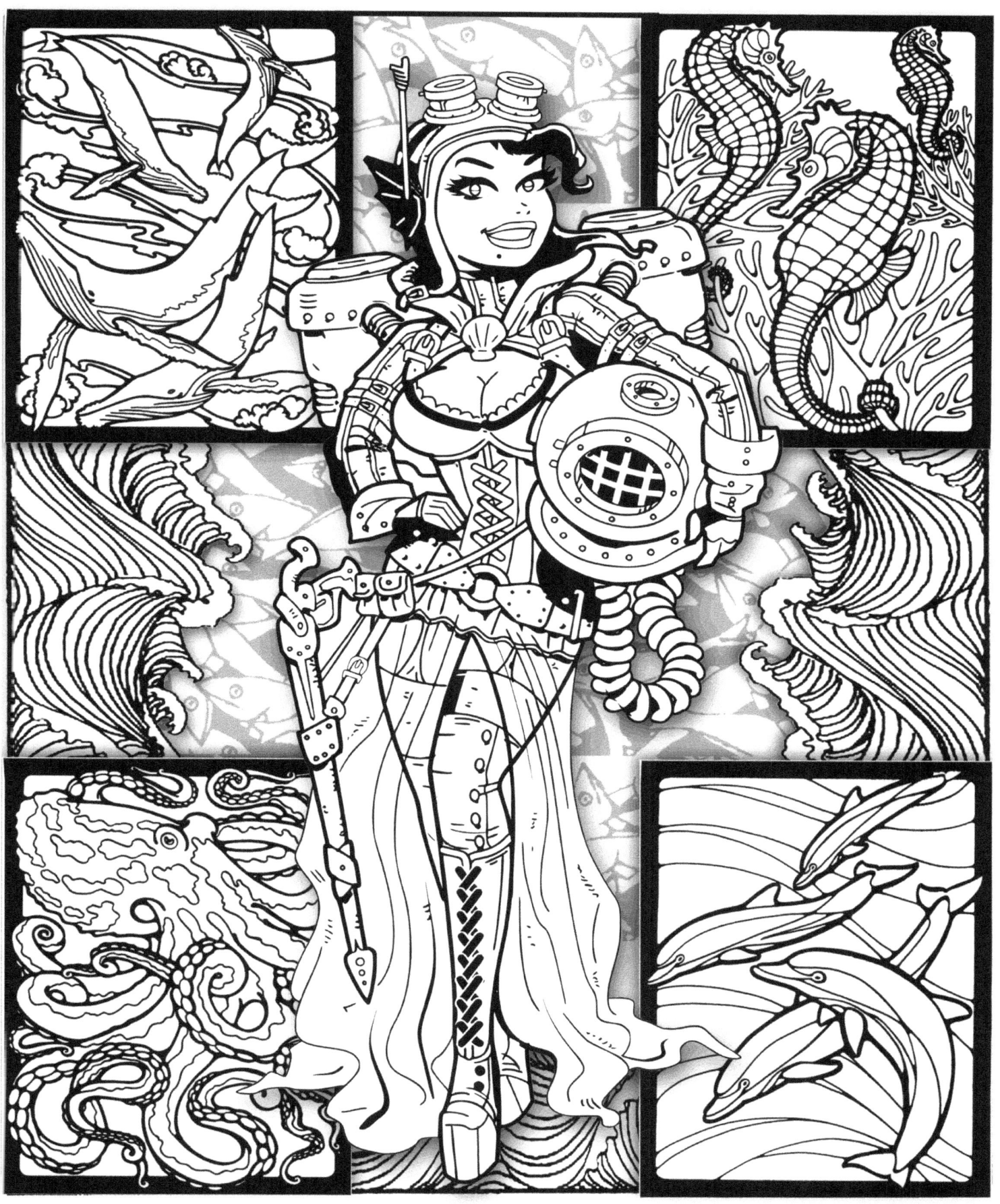

This page is intentionally left blank to prevent marker bleed through, and to let you remove your colored page on the reverse side for display

FANNY

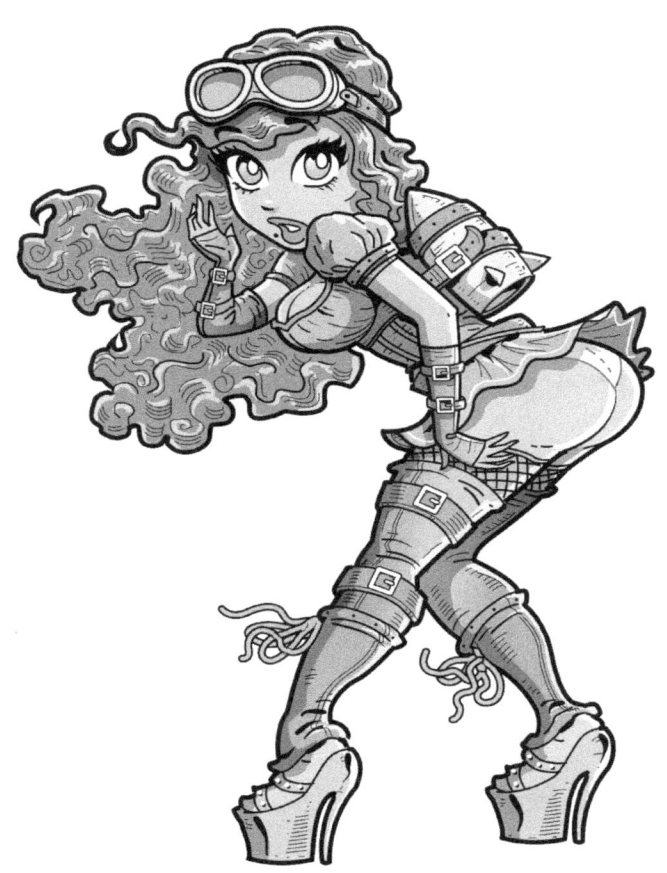

FANNY

"The rocket pack, out of combustium, would be of no further assistance in making an escape. Fanny turned and saw that the cutthroats were almost upon her. Fortunately, she still had two weapons in reserve.

She deployed the first by bending at the waist, stunning her attackers with an unfettered view of her backside as she drew a shining object from her shoe.

"They always look at the derriere," she laughed to herself, "instead of the derringer."

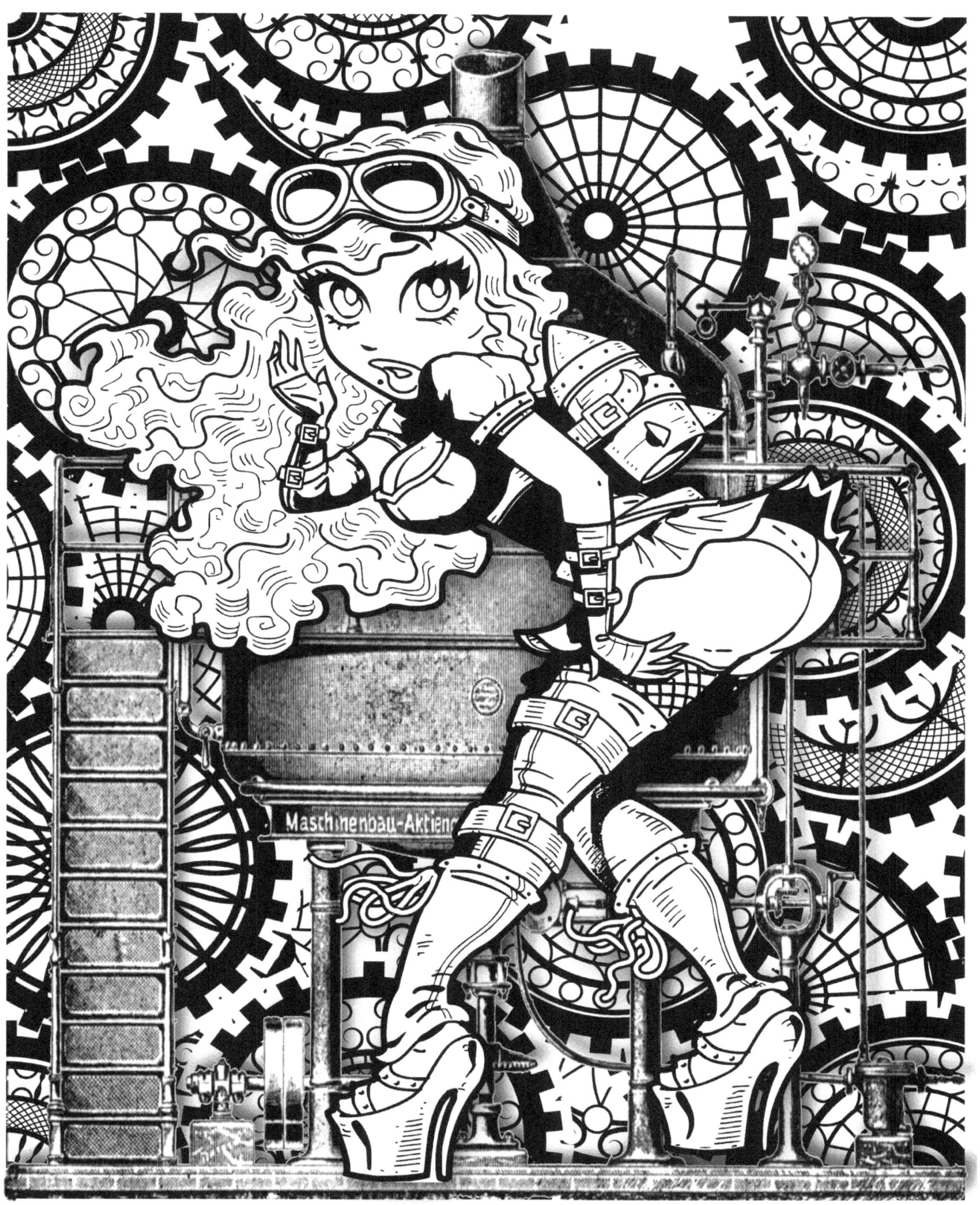

This page is intentionally left blank to prevent marker bleed through, and to let you remove your colored page on the reverse side for display

Genevieve

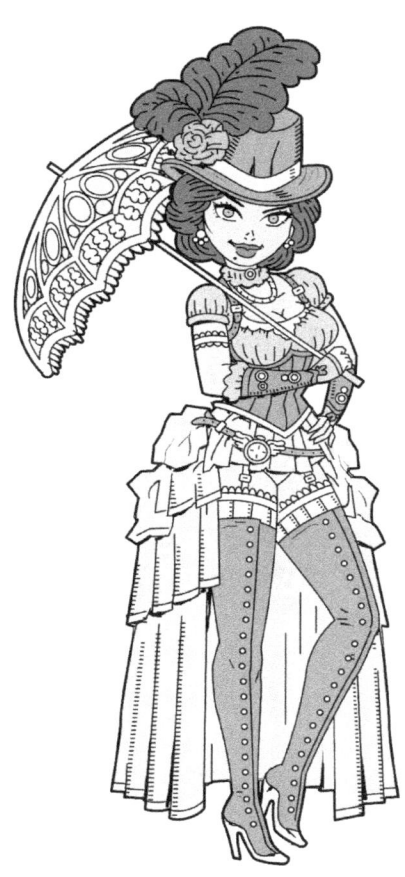

GENEVIEVE

"Your quarters are inescapable, yes," said the Commandant, "But how can you call this a prison? Luxuries abound! Consider it rather a gilded cage designed to prevent the flight of a rare and, may I say, beautiful bird."

"Birds of prey are not meant to be contained," Genevieve said as she slipped the concealed sword from her parasol.

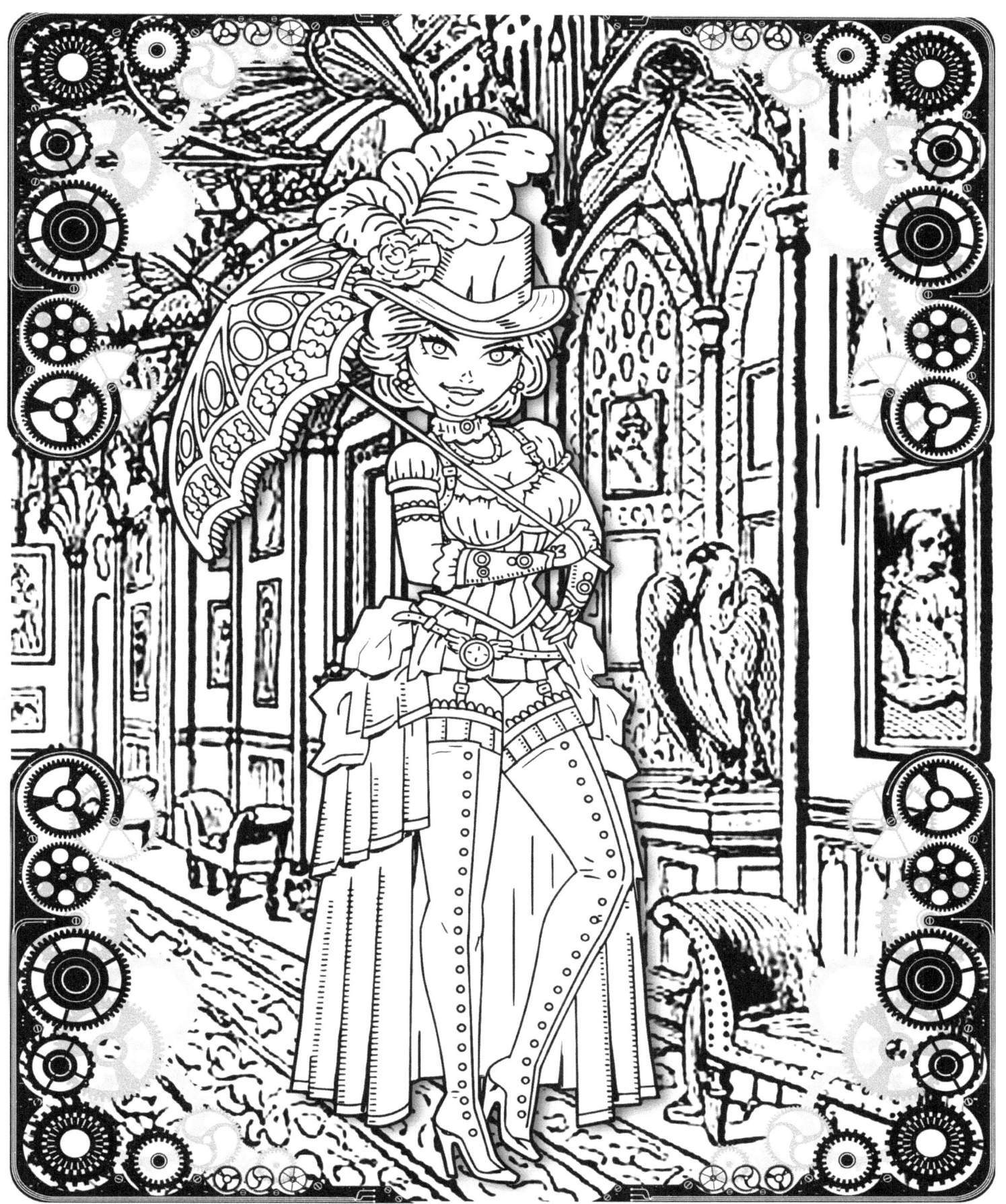

This page is intentionally left blank to prevent marker bleed through,
and to let you remove your colored page on the reverse side for display

Constance

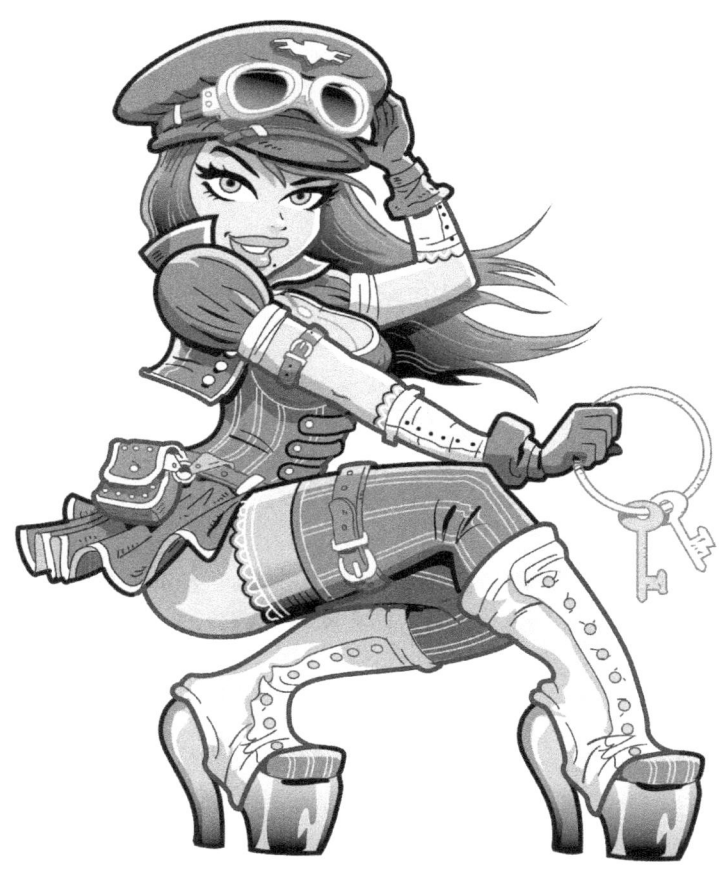

CONSTANCE

"I TOLD YOU I'D BE BACK!" CONSTANCE SHOUTED AS SHE OPENED THE CELL DOOR.

HER CREW MEMBERS STUMBLED OUT OF THE DARKNESS, ALTERNATELY SHIELDING THEIR EYES FROM THE BLINDING DAYLIGHT AND GLANCING WARILY AT THE APPROACHING LEVIATHAN.

"NO TIME FOR EXPLANATIONS," SHE BARKED. "FOLLOW ME TO THE AIRSHIP AND PREPARE TO DO BATTLE FOR EARTH ITSELF!"

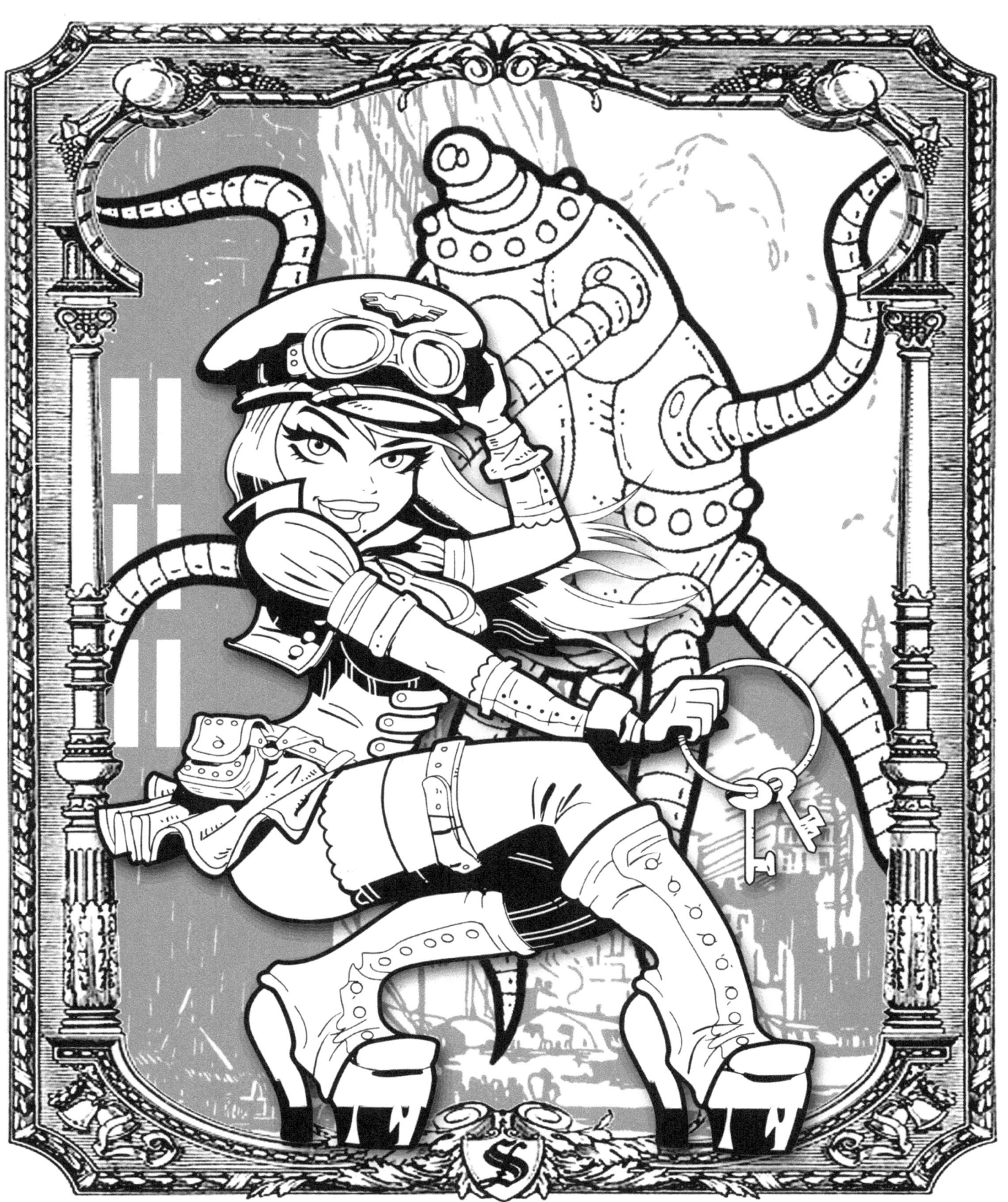

This page is intentionally left blank to prevent marker bleed through, and to let you remove your colored page on the reverse side for display

CHASTITY

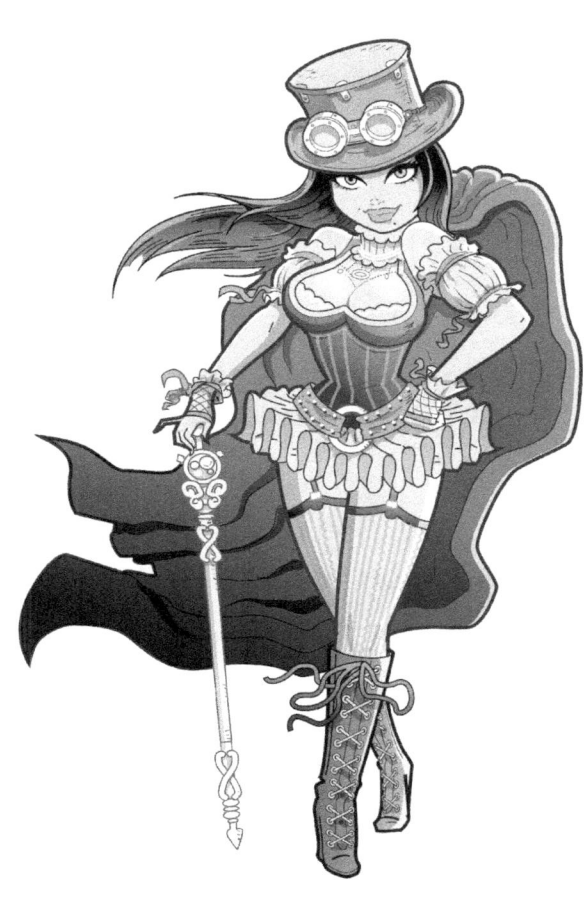

CHASTITY

"RATHER CUMBERSOME FOR A MUSIC BOX, ISN'T IT?" RIVET HEAD GROWLED OVER THE MECHANIZED MELODY. HE APPROACHED MENACINGLY, WITH MURDER IN HIS EYES.

"CALL IT AN INDULGENCE," CHASTITY REPLIED, "BUT I FIND DANCING AND FIGHTING ARE BOTH MORE PLEASURABLE WITH MUSICAL ACCOMPANIMENT."

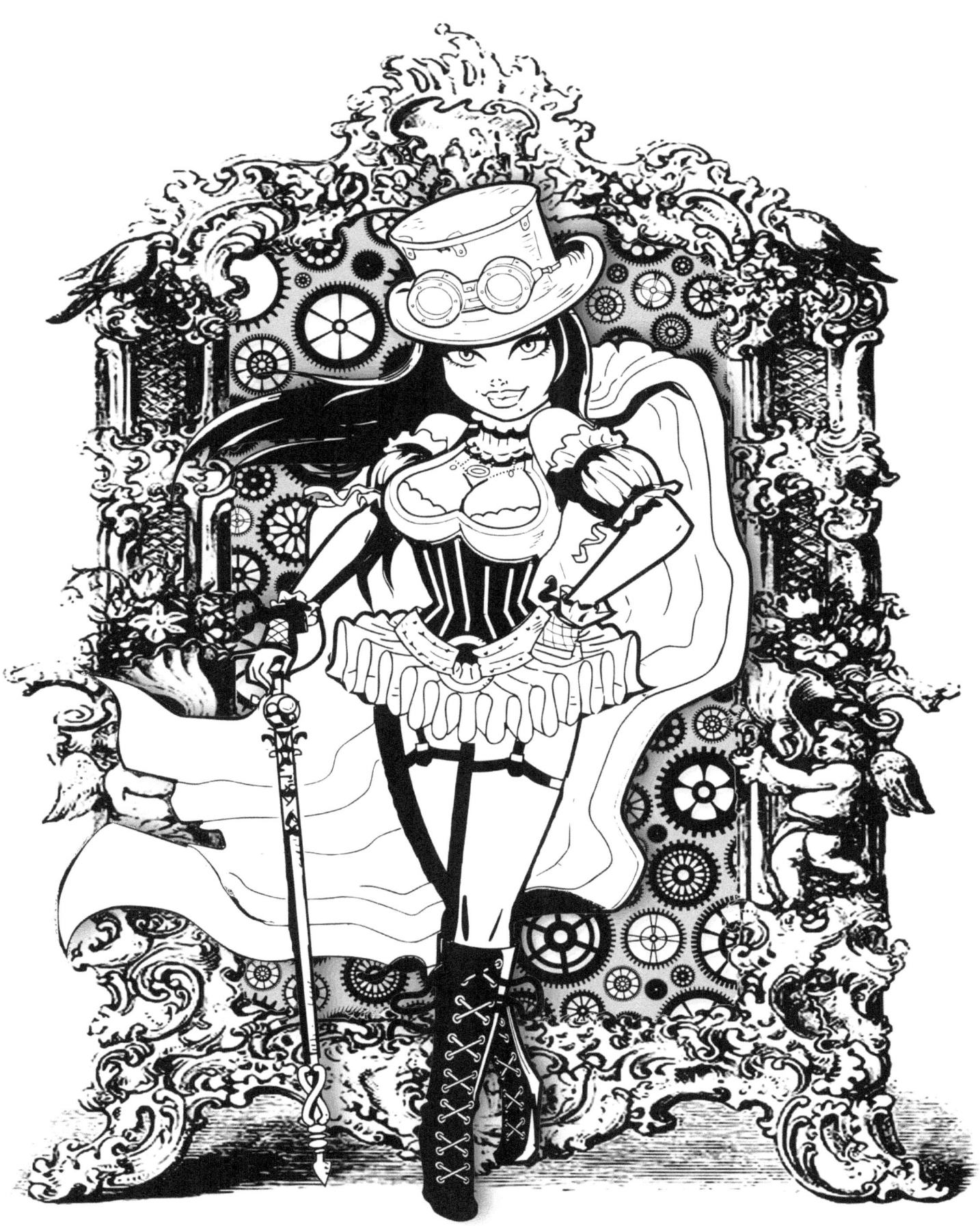

This page is intentionally left blank to prevent marker bleed through,
and to let you remove your colored page on the reverse side for display

MOLLY

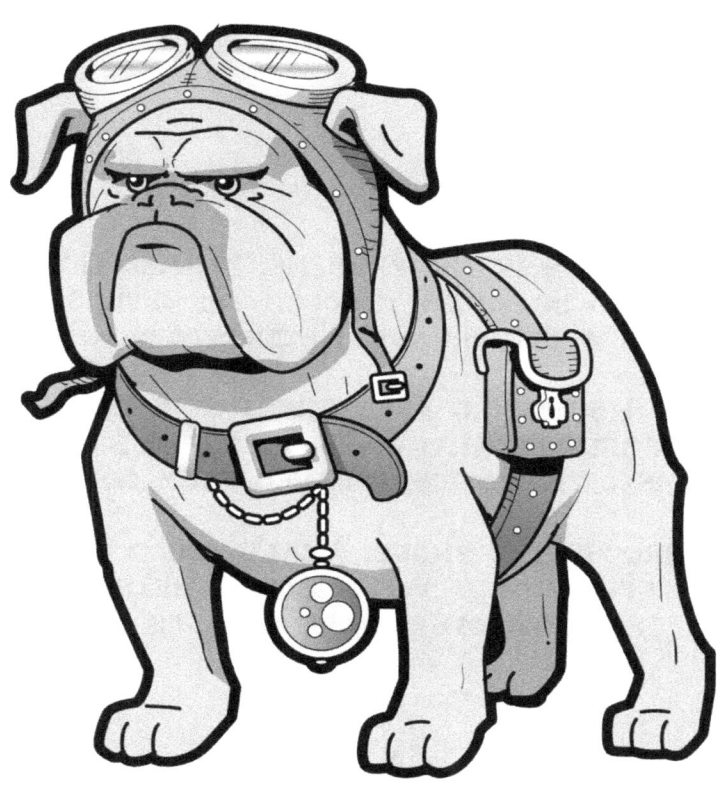

MOLLY

THE SCENE WAS NIGHTMARISH IN THE EXTREME. FLAMES LICKED THE NIGHT SKY AND THICK SMOKE WHIRLED IN EDDIES THROUGH THE DEBRIS-FILLED STREET. THE TOWERING CAT WAS A JUGGERNAUT. NEVER STOPPING AND DEVOID OF MERCY.

SUDDENLY, THE AIR WAS SUNDERED BY A GREAT SCREECHING SOUND AS GEARS CLASHED AND TORE THEMSELVES APART. THE MONSTER SHUDDERED TO A HALT, AND THE HELLISH BEAMS OF LIGHT DISAPPEARED FROM ITS EYES.

AND THAT'S WHEN, THROUGH THE SMOKE, MOLLY COULD BE SEEN STANDING ASTRIDE THE BEAST, BATTERED BUT VICTORIOUS. WHETHER SHE DEFEATED THE INFERNAL MECHANICAL FELINE THROUGH NATURAL INSTINCT OR THE PROVENANCE OF A MERCIFUL GOD, WHO CAN SAY?

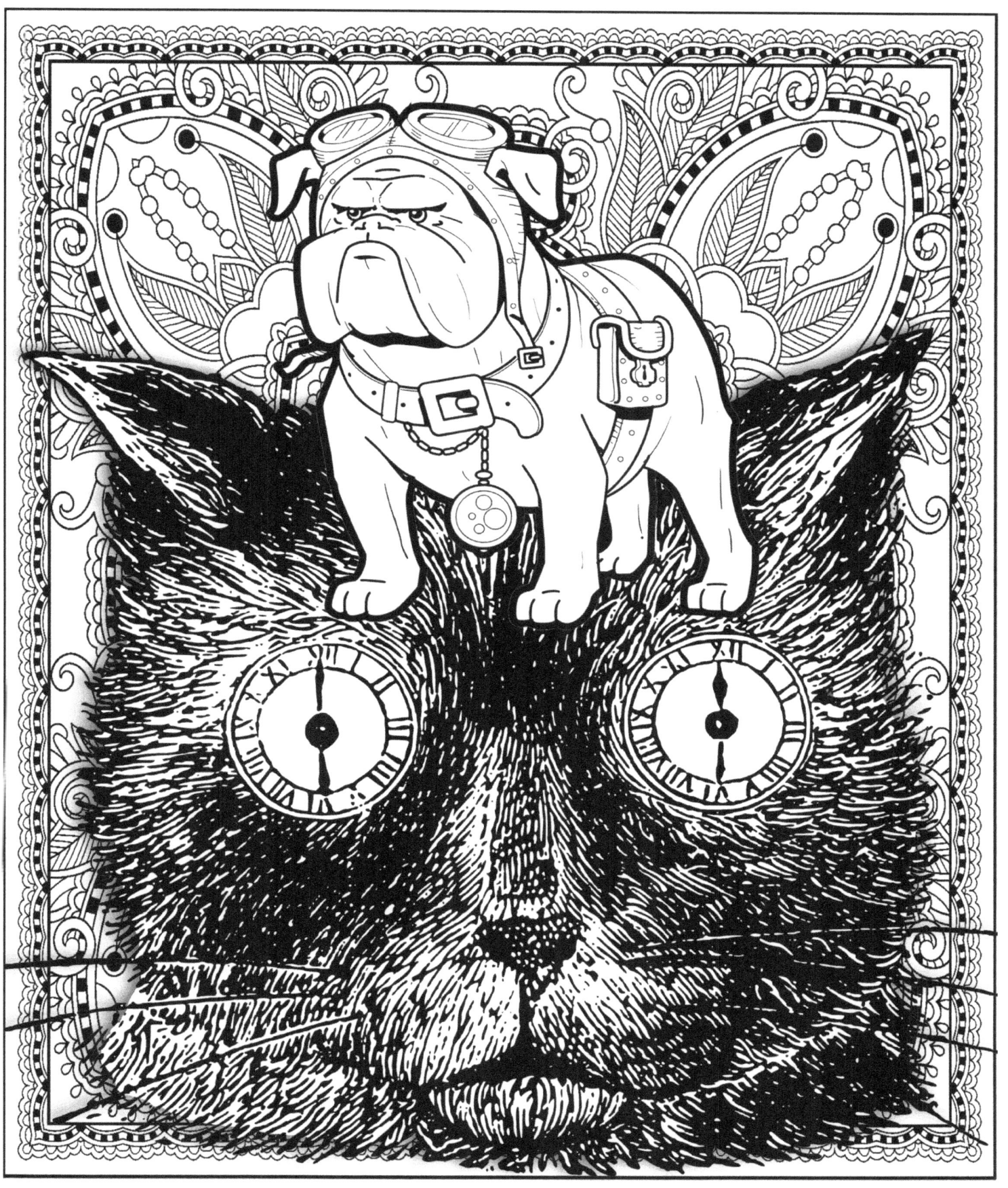